PAVEMENT

Rustin Larson

Blue Light Press ❖ 1st World Publishing

1st WORLD
PUBLISHING

San Francisco ❖ Fairfield ❖ Delhi

WINNER OF THE **2016** BLUE LIGHT POETRY PRIZE

PAVEMENT

Copyright ©2017 by Rustin Larson

1ST WORLD LIBRARY
PO Box 2211
Fairfield, IA 52556
www.1stworldpublishing.com

BLUE LIGHT PRESS
www.bluelightpress.com
Email: bluelightpress@aol.com

BOOK & COVER DESIGN
Melanie Gendron
www.melaniegendron.com

COVER PHOTOGRAPH
Rustin Larson

AUTHOR PHOTOGRAPH
Galen Watt

FIRST EDITION

ISBN 978-1-4218-3778-9

PRAISE FOR RUSTIN LARSON'S POETRY

Even for Rustin Larson, a master of invention, *Pavement* breaks into new territory. *"This aquarium / I swim in every day / funded in part by / the Martian government. . ."* I love the images he chooses, where he goes with them, and the way he transforms them. *"a dance I attend / only in my imagination / and then only / as 2nd alto sax. . ."* So much in these lines and so much underneath them. *"an otherwise blackened / stage within which / the dance of the silver / gypsies begins."* Brilliant writing, a delight on every page, a joy to read! *"the celestial City / of Wonders / thrown open coldly, / but / with such pulsing beauty."*

—Diane Frank, Author of
    Canon for Bears and Ponderosa Pines

Challenging a reader's perspective while remaining accessible, direct and vulnerable, Rustin Larson magically turns the routine into the extraordinary. His ability to craft memories, whether shaded, flickering or luminous, entices readers of *Bum Cantos, Winter Jazz, & The Collected Discography of Morning* to linger, examine and encounter the significance of seemingly routine lives. Larson elegantly uses detailed, sensual images, chiming rhythms, and well-chosen, well-placed words to evoke layers of thematic content. Rustin Larson's poems entertain and inform while examining the many facets of the lives we endeavor to accept, enjoy and use for good purpose.

—Michael Carrino, Author of *By Available Light*

Larson writes like an angel, but one who's willing to work both sides of the street.

—John Peterson, *Wapsipinicon Almanac*

Like Odysseus, Larson has been trying to find his way home, or at least to redefine that home. Larson's vehicle for his journey is the process of writing itself, which he has dedicated himself to and which he knows can be both circuitous and serendipitous. But the writer who pursues his craft, like Odysseus who pursues the journey home, must have patience. . . the poet and his journey are one.

—Stephen Schneider, *Pirene's Fountain*

Each poem in Larson's book is packed with as much detail as a short story. The narrator often alludes to literary works, famous as well as infamous people, easily identifiable locations on the globe, and renowned historical events that either relate to the poems thematically, or place the memories in history for the reader. The poems do not adhere to any one form, but rather, they take form as their contents require. Larson's writing style is multifarious.

—Stephen Page, *Buenos Aires Herald*

From moment to moment, Larson is surrealistic, Proustian, stand-up-comedy funny, dead serious, sad, ecstatic, deadpan. In Larson's multitude of stories and modes, there's always some layer of the writer concerned with craft, with metawriting. . . Write on, Rustin, write on.

—Vince Gotera, *North American Review*

Rustin Larson wrote these poems, while wearing a grease stained tee shirt. I wish to buy this guy a collection of fat notebooks, because I want him to keep writing. By the way, he does not know that the cricket crawling up his leg, wants a taste of the ice cream sandwich he ate yesterday. He'll share, he always does. How do I know? I know, because, he's so generous. If you're from Ottumwa, you got it, and don't need to read these poems. Otherwise, buy this book, or you'll never know how to put bat wings on a minivan.

—Ibu Robin Lim, Author of *The Geometry of Splitting Souls*

ACKNOWLEDGMENTS

PAVEMENT 1 (Poets/Artists)

PAVEMENT 4 (Briar Cliff Review)

PAVEMENT 5 (Poets/Artists)

PAVEMENT 6 (Saranac Review)

PAVEMENT 7 (Poets/Artists)

PAVEMENT 12 (Pirene's Fountain)

PAVEMENT 13 (Midway Journal)

CONTENTS

PAVEMENT 1

                                          Hungry, I make my way
to the crock
            of barley soup
                  at the health market
on Independence.

          What I'm seeing
               in the sky
is not a missile
            but a jet liner
                banking in approach
into National.
          The traffic is dense.

I find a seat
           at the window,
              read first the legitimate
and then the underground
            papers. At times it feels
                like a college town
here on Capitol Hill.
         I'm a student
              of something.
I've forgotten.

A fellow
           with a yellow beard
              and a bathrobe
smells of

           weeks old urine…

         But before long
the clerk is shoving him

out the door
and then running to the bathroom
to wash her hands.

He stumbles

into the flow
of foot traffic,
gets swept.

A job,

a place to live.

Lyricism in the
misfortune
of the doomed.

Don't kid yourself.

PAVEMENT 2

Kid, I really don't
                know how you're doing.
                        All I know is
every flower
                tries to kill you,
                            so you
                must flee, and we are
                            left without your
long-stemmed grace
                & goofiness
                            we need like a drink.

A lot of dangerous
                confessions;

I'll stick

                with the longest one,
                            the most elegant,
most like you
                in a silver dress
                            at a dance I attend
only in my imagination,
                and then only
                            as 2nd alto sax
in a jazz choir
                playing
                            Stomping at the Savoy.

What wouldn't a whole
                pile of everybody give
                            to make this place

safe for your rarity,

to watch you glide
        in the weather from
                the comfort of our own eye glasses.

I watch my hand
                    worrying in pencil.
If it weren't so
      I wouldn't be here.
        But I'd rather have
the honor
      to watch you pay
        for my lunch
again anytime,
      you lyrical beauty.
        I'd rather have that
than words.

PAVEMENT 3

This aquarium
I swim in every day
            funded in part by
                        the Martian government
would make
            me a fish of relatively
                        general interest.

My own game warden

in these parts, I don't
                        know what the younger
            lights in the sky, the weeds
or the rabid dogs
think of me now.
It's been 30 years since
I was a beginner and
I think a second
            cornet in the marching
                        band. Yet, they still
recommend an aspirin
            a day for me, my
                        blood platelets being
so sticky and all.
            So they make me run
                        on a treadmill
until I'm almost
            actually dying

and
                        they slap me
            down on a table
                        stick a cold stethoscope

on my chest and listen
          to the wild jazzy
                    rhythms of Radio Rustin.

Funny. People
                    I've always
          been leery of never call.
They've
                    got good reason now.
Writing close
                    to home is never a good idea
                    unless you mean to
          get drunk with everyone
                    and play that strange
arm wrestling game
          where you tether
a scorpion to the table
and the loser gets
a nasty sting. They love
                    that game at family reunions.
I've been working out.
          I hate to lose.

To say I meant
          no harm is not
                    quite entirely true.

And yet people,
          there are some nights
                    when the crickets
are chirping
          and the sun is
                    a dissolving
red lozenge
          on the tongue
                    of nightfall

when I say quit it—
                    we are all just this.
                              I'd give you my
last marshmallow
                  if I had one.
                              I'm so peculiar
about these things.
                I know I can't escape
                              from myself, but I've
known a few people
                I'd give my lungs to.
                        I know this doesn't
exonerate me, but
                shit. Let the cat in.
                    It's cold outside.

PAVEMENT 4

Things that made us
        feel at home:
                playing with matches,
playing with the plastic
        Indians lit ablaze,
          chanting a war cry
      as the flame made
          a pearl of the face,
the headdress...   The
        howl of the coyote
           in the dark passageway
between the garage
      and the potato field,
        the mark of a claw
on our back door,
      the frost on concrete
        in the moonlight,
the stubborn
      witchlike curl
        of trees in fog,
the pancakes of apology,
      the loose gravel
           that skidded you out
into the skin graft unit,
      the nightmare of tin
          buckets full of chicken
heads, the railroad
        ties piled near
the garage, the slivers
      of space the diamond-
         back corn snakes slithered
the non-poisonous
      but deadly

congratulations from
the neighbor's mom,
her small glass
of grain alcohol
and
her cigarette ready
to catch the world

ablaze, the repeated
advice of crows
high in the barkless
tree,
the passage of the sun
across the surface
of our skulls,
the crescendo
of squad cars
chasing a Harley
down 9th,
the shocked burst
of a car through
the picket fence
on the cul-de-sac,
the fighter jets ripping
toward some invisible
enemy, the coolness
of evening grasping
your bare arms like orderlies
at the sanitorium, the electric
shock therapy
of streetlights suddenly
igniting, their lone
spots of surveillance
lit like circles

on an otherwise blackened
          stage within which
the dance of the silver
gypsies begins.

PAVEMENT 5

The pallbearer
          has a rat's tongue,
                    but a suit crisp
as a new 50 dollar bill.
          To tell you the truth,
                    the coffin is way too
heavy for a weakling
          like me, but I carry
                    anyway, knowing
the ride for this corpse
          is going to throw
                    my back out something major.
But it's a trip to The Stone
          tonight for a six
                    of stout and I'll leave
the cigarettes alone—
          maybe a bag of beef
                    jerky for the pug.
She made a special
          request anyway.
                    The western light hits
the trees and I think
          of you, probably dinner-
                    time in Garlic-
ville, some roasted
          salmon and a plate
                    of sliced tomatoes. No
big deal to have you
          inside me all the time
                    sitting on the sofa (
my pancreas) with your arm
          around my conscience.
                    I get along pretty well

with the trees.
       The sun makes them look
                    so clean and cheerful.
I'll probably stay right here
            until midnight and
                      watch their slow,
mysterious disappearance.
             You know, I could
                      call you, but I like
the dialogue of silence.
           It's like most me
                   in the mirror
                        of myself,

and I'll notice nothing
except eventually
            in the blackness there'll be
                     the cricket crawling carefully
and closely up my leg
          to stay warm.

PAVEMENT 6

The meter and shape
            of his lines were
                        determined
by the width
            of the notebook.
            He'd drive around
the city for hours
            in a green 1964 Beetle,
                        looking for the ultimate
glint of sun
                        off the buildings. He worshipped
            snow at dusk,
the purple stripes crusting
            the roadsides,
                        the cawing of crows
he couldn't see. It was
            near the sculpture garden
                        he'd sit and he could
                                    barely make out the
words,
but she, at least,
            was beautiful
in his mind, he knew
                        she always would be,
            Quan Yin, the goddess
                        of compassion, whom
he knew and whom
            he would meet again,
                        the starlight gaining
thirstily above him,
            the celestial City
of Wonders
            thrown open coldly,
but
            with such pulsing beauty.

PAVEMENT 7

Disappearances.

The Dodo.
        Jimmy Hoffa.
                Nameless in
Alabama, Argentina.
                        Large mushroom and black
olive pizzas.   Glaciers.
        Atlantis. Shangri La.
            Washington's
teeth. Childhood.
        Sparky
                 the goldfish. Amelia
Earhart. The Titanic.
        Ambrose Bierce. Spalding
           Gray.

Announcing he
        had made a new
              decision, he climbed
inside his blue Ford Galaxy
        and neither he nor
           the car was seen again.
The earth just don't
        open up and swallow
           folk, now do it?   Tiny
clouds. Small hills
        of dust. Who notices
           them anyway?
Some people disappear
        inside themselves.
           The window won't open.

A year passes. But then again,
          some people just
                              invent new names for
Things. Nothing really
            disappears. Where
                              would it all go anyway?
Where would it fit?

PAVEMENT 8

Hearing voices.
      When I know it's from
           the TV or the radio
with the volume dimmed
      to nil, that's one thing;
          what prophecies
can I divine from mis-
      heard
          grain futures?
I rake leaves
      and the sun whispers
          phonemes of wind. Save,
it seems to hiss. Save,
      save all you can.

PAVEMENT 9

In this dream
        you are unhappy
            because the gift of furniture
you received from your dad
        won't fit into the packing crate
          of an apartment
you've chosen to rent.
        So I'm trailing behind
           you and some of your
lady friends, listening
        to you despair: "Every-
          thing works out
for my sister, but never for me."
           You pause to rest
on a stone bench
          near a Rose of Sharon,
and I bend down
        to hug you, my hand
          behind your cool neck,
and I press our foreheads
        together.

          Nothing needs to be said.

I let go.
       You begin walking again;
         gradually you fade.

I find myself
       touching
        wet leaves.

It's growing darker.
         I fade
into my life again.

PAVEMENT 10

It was a great idea,
            putting wings
on the minivan
            so we could fly
above the natural disasters
                        in our escape
west to the plateaus
            where the breathable
                        air lingered.
It came in handy
            to jump that massive
                        lava flow in South
Dakota—It's just
            sad the Capuchin
                        got so keyed up
she jumped out the open
            window and
                        disappeared
in a crispy flash.
            There's nothing like the stink
                        of barbecued monkey,
which, thank God,
            we didn't smell because
                        we were flying
with those great improvised
            bat wings made of old
                        tents and the skeletons
of lawn furniture.
            If our DNA survives
                        this trip
we will be deemed
            the progenitors of the new
                        world, I suppose.

But really, it just takes
           a little spit and know-how.
                  It could be anybody.

PAVEMENT 11

The most popular mask
        of course was
                the cobalt blue one that
had been coated with
        feathers and
                split down the center
with a jigsaw.
        So many people saw
                themselves in this,
and a few even tried
        it on, reporting they
                experienced an absolute
severance between
        the self
and the ego, and
                that 80% of their
thought processes was
        now stellar dust.

PAVEMENT 12

It is raining in Des
       Moines, September.
              We disembark
and the bus gasps and pulls
       away. We are pushing
           open the door
of the "Oriental Market."
      At the cash register a cone
           of incense burns
in the gut of Buddha;
      The fragrance is like
           no flower I've ever
smelled, but insists,
      I am sure, the holds
           of ships, spilled
containers of saffron,
      and secreted casks
           of opium. There are
posters of red splashed
      with gold Chinese
           calligraphy. There
are pictures of odd
      mountains eaten away
           by mists of sulfuric
acid. You thumb
      through the silk blouses
           embroidered with dragons
or flowers or circular symbols
      for luck, sex and
           prosperity. I touch
the small colorful
      boxes of rice candy—
           the sweet amber cubes

plugged at the cardboard
        flap by a tiny plastic
                race car or half-naked
baby. The woman
       at the cash register eyes us
              as she smokes. She
was beautiful once.
        Her red silk blouse,
if you look
       carefully,
            tells the story
of the Cruel Prince
       and the Phoenix
            and the Celestial Dynasty.
We make our purchases,
      I with coins I've
            been saving all month,
coins that are cast on
       the counter: mysterious
            fortune, long life,
but much travail. She
       blows smoke over my
            head in a blessing
as the money drawer
       rolls and the
            chimes resound.

PAVEMENT 13

Norfolk Island Pine,
            part of you drinks
                        sunlight.
Is this why you
            slouch like a drunk
                        or an overworked
accountant?

                        The emerald green
skywalk carpeting
            you stand upon
                        is nothing in comparison
to the way gold
            illuminates you from
                        inside
            as if
inebriation
            were all that mattered.
                        But you've got a living
to make, branches
            the copper color of
                        death
to slough off
            someday,
but not
            now, not here.
                        I suspect I am
just like you, a wanderer
            stuck in a pot
                        the color of bricks
with the wind of foot traffic
            being the only
                        thing stirring

my worry there won't
                be navy bean soup
                                or money to pay
the light bulbs. Yeah, we
                could drink together;
                                you could tell me
about your life
                as a seedling
in Ottumwa,
                                how all the other
seedlings laughed
                at you when you
                                said you were going
to make it and not
                be stuck staring
                                at some wild
sexy sycamore
                through a pane
                                of glass the rest
of your life.

PAVEMENT 14

No one pledges allegiance
            to pavement.
                        Motorcycles buzz down
its neck, flatten a generation
            of beer cans.
18 wheelers
                        head up
its spinal chord;
    flashes of nightfall
                        fire
the cricket's song;
            lone transmission tower
                        blinks up,
down, up, down: It is here;
            the middle
                        of nowhere.

ABOUT THE AUTHOR

Rustin Larson's poetry has appeared in *The New Yorker, The Iowa Review, North American Review, Poetry East, Saranac Review, Poets & Artists* and other magazines.   He is the author of *The Wine-Dark House* (Blue Light Press, 2009) and *Crazy Star* (selected for the Loess Hills Book's Poetry Series in 2005). Larson won 1st Editor's Prize from *Rhino Magazine* in 2000 and has won prizes for his poetry from The National Poet Hunt and The Chester H. Jones Foundation among others. A seven-time Pushcart nominee, and graduate of the Vermont College MFA in Writing, Larson was an Iowa Poet at The Des Moines National Poetry Festival in 2002 & 2004, a featured writer in the DMACC Celebration of the Literary Arts in 2007 & 2008, and he was a featured poet at the Poetry at Round Top Festival in May 2012.

www.ingramcontent.com/pod-product-compliance
Lightning Source LLC
Chambersburg PA
CBHW021917040426

42447CB00007B/903